I Wonder Why

Planes Have Wings

and Other Questions About Transportation

Chris Maynard

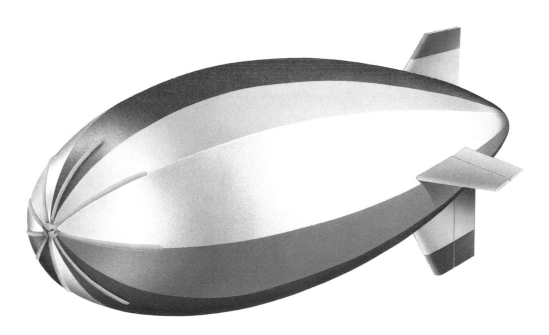

Kingfisher Books

NEW YORK

KINGFISHER BOOKS
Grisewood & Dempsey Inc.
95 Madison Avenue
New York, New York 10016

First American edition 1993
10 9 8 7 6 5 4 3 2 1
Copyright © Grisewood & Dempsey Ltd. 1993

Library of Congress Cataloging-in-Publication Data
Maynard, Christopher.
    I wonder why planes have wings and other questions
about transportation/by Chris Maynard. —1st American
ed.
        p.   cm.
    Includes index.
    Summary: Answers questions about transportation
and vehicles, including "Do airships run on air?" and
"Why don't ships sink?"
    1. Aeronautics — Miscellanea — Juvenile literature.
2. Motor vehicles — Miscellanea — Juvenile literature.
3. Ships — Miscellanea — Juvenile literature.
4. Transportation — Miscellanea — Juvenile literature.
[1.Transportation — Miscellanea.   2. Vehicles —
Miscellanea.   3. Questions and answers.]   I Title.
TL547.M443 1993
629.04—dc20   92-42373 CIP AC

ISBN 1-85697-877-X
Printed in Italy

Series editor: Jackie Gaff
Series designer: David West Children's Books
Author: Chris Maynard
Consultant: Ian Graham
Editor: Brigid Avison
Art editor: Christina Fraser
Cover illustrations: Chris Forsey, cartoons by
    Tony Kenyon (B.L. Kearley Ltd)
Illustrations: Chris Forsey pp. 4-7, 16-21, 26 (wagon train),
    28-9; Tony Kenyon (B.L. Kearley) all cartoons;
    Sebastian Quigley (Linden Artists) pp. 10-11, 26-7
    (train); Stephen Seymour (Bernard Thornton Artists)
    pp. 30-1 (aircraft); Ian Thompson pp. 8-9, 12-13; Ross
    Watton (Garden Studio) pp. 14-15, 22-5, 30
    (transporter), 31 (ships).

CONTENTS

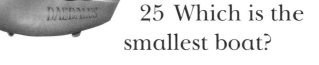

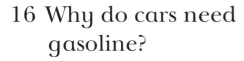

How far can I go in an hour?

If you keep walking for an hour, and don't stop to take any rests, your own two legs will carry you about 2½ miles (4 km). You'll be able to go farther if you run, but you'll probably have to keep stopping to get your breath back. The easiest way to travel more than a few miles in an hour is to get something to carry you!

- It would take an ordinary garden snail more than three days to get as far as you can walk in one hour.

- Trotting on a pony for an hour, you'd be able to travel three times as far as you would on foot.

- To walk as far as a jumbo jet can carry you in an hour, you'd have to keep going for more than ten whole days and nights!

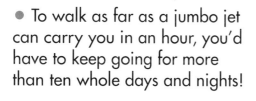

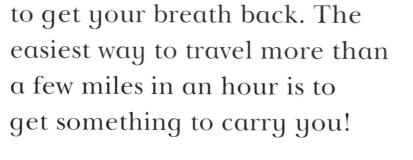

- Racing cyclists can pedal at least ten times as fast as you can walk. They can go as far as 25 miles (40 km) in an hour.

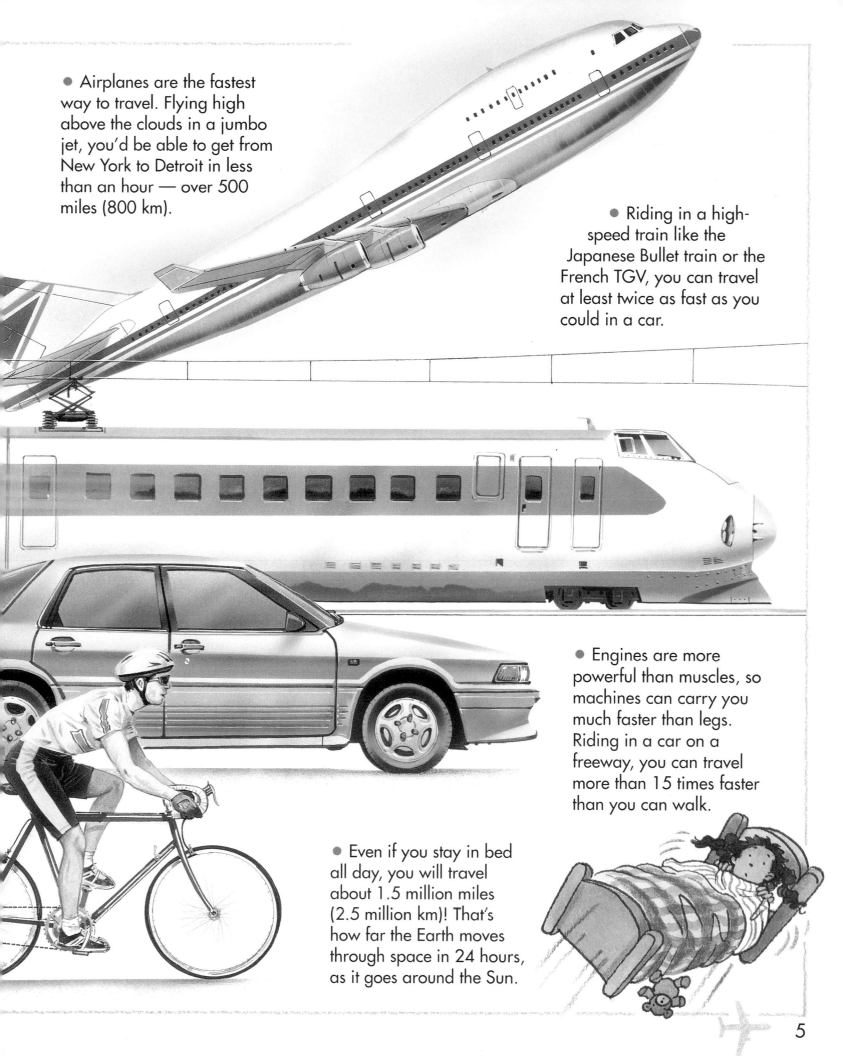

● Airplanes are the fastest way to travel. Flying high above the clouds in a jumbo jet, you'd be able to get from New York to Detroit in less than an hour — over 500 miles (800 km).

● Riding in a high-speed train like the Japanese Bullet train or the French TGV, you can travel at least twice as fast as you could in a car.

● Engines are more powerful than muscles, so machines can carry you much faster than legs. Riding in a car on a freeway, you can travel more than 15 times faster than you can walk.

● Even if you stay in bed all day, you will travel about 1.5 million miles (2.5 million km)! That's how far the Earth moves through space in 24 hours, as it goes around the Sun.

Which is the fastest car?

A British car called *Thrust 2* set the world land speed record in 1983. Using an aircraft jet engine in place of a normal car engine, it reached nearly 634 miles an hour (1,020 km/h).

- The first car to go faster than 60 miles an hour (100 km/h) was battery-powered. It was called *La Jamais Contente*, and it did this nearly 100 years ago, in 1899.

- The world's fastest sailing craft are sailboards. In good winds, they can zip across the water at more than 50 miles an hour (80 km/h).

Spirit of Australia

Which is the fastest boat?

Hydroplanes skim over the water almost as if flying. In 1977, Ken Warby roared to 345 miles an hour (556 km/h) in his jet-powered *Spirit of Australia*.

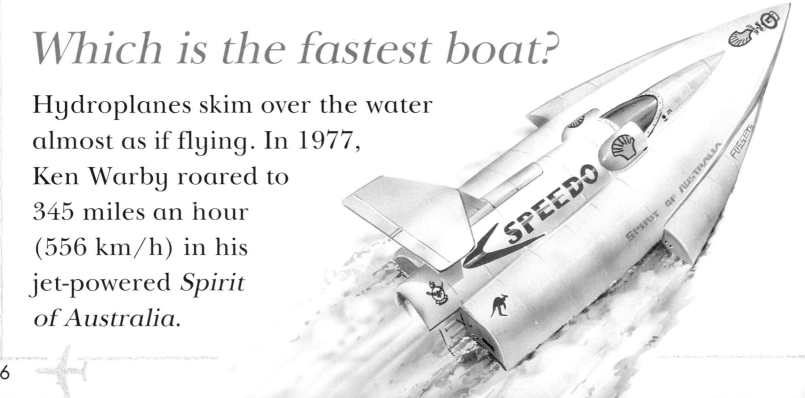

Thrust 2

● To carry astronauts to the Moon in the 1960s and 1970s, the Saturn-Apollo rockets had to travel more than 40 times as fast as a jumbo jet. But the top speed of the astronauts' moon buggy was only 10 miles an hour (16 km/h)!

SR-71A *Blackbird*

● One of the quickest ways to travel without an engine is on skis.

Which is the fastest jet plane?

The official world record speed for jet airplanes was set back in 1976, when a Lockheed SR-71A reached an amazing 2,193 miles an hour (3,530 km/h)! It was nicknamed *Blackbird*.

Why do planes have wings?

Planes have wings for the same reason that birds do — to help them to fly.

Plane wings work because of their shape. They are curved more on top than underneath, and this makes air flow faster above them than below. The faster air above the wings sucks them upward!

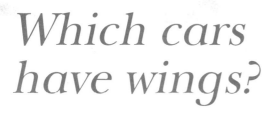

• To see how wings work, blow hard over the top of a piece of thin paper. The paper will rise up!

Which cars have wings?

Racing cars such as dragsters have wings — upside-down ones, curved more underneath than on top. They work in the opposite way to plane wings, sucking down instead of up, to help the tires grip the track.

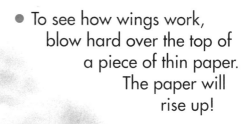

Wing

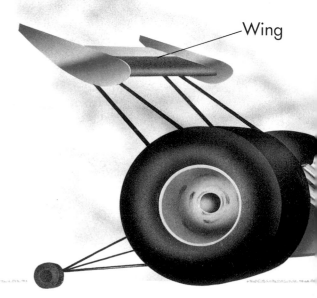

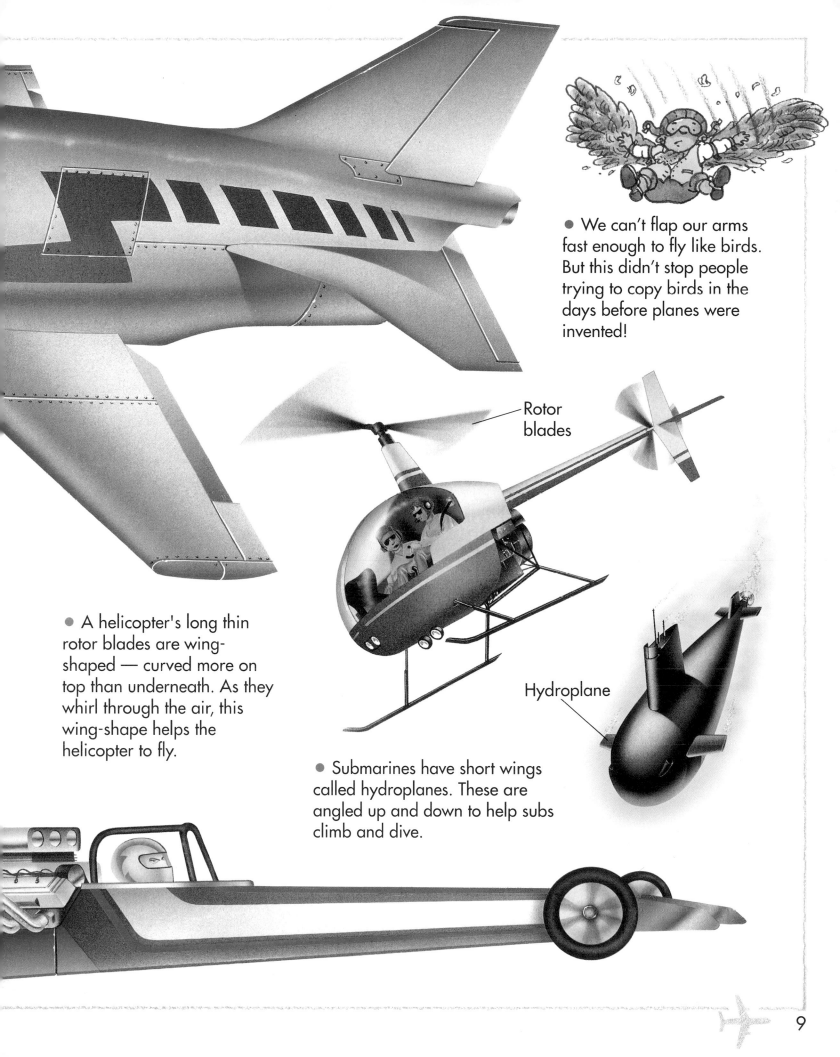

- We can't flap our arms fast enough to fly like birds. But this didn't stop people trying to copy birds in the days before planes were invented!

Rotor blades

- A helicopter's long thin rotor blades are wing-shaped — curved more on top than underneath. As they whirl through the air, this wing-shape helps the helicopter to fly.

Hydroplane

- Submarines have short wings called hydroplanes. These are angled up and down to help subs climb and dive.

Which plane can wiggle its nose?

The superfast passenger jet Concorde can move its nose. With its long slim nose sticking straight out, Concorde can slip through the air at well over double the speed of a jumbo jet. However, when Concorde lands, its nose has to be lowered out of the way. If this isn't done, the pilot can't see the runway!

● Concorde heats up so much in flight that its body stretches — it can get as much as 11 inches (28 cm) longer.

● The world's largest passenger planes, the Boeing 747s, are nicknamed jumbo jets after an elephant. Jumbo was a star attraction at the Barnum and Bailey circus in the 1880s.

Can planes swing their wings?

Yes, some fighter planes have wings that can be moved in and out. This is because wings that stick straight out are the best shape for taking off and landing, and for flying slowly. When wings swing back, they give the plane a smoother shape, which helps it to cut through the air at top speed.

● Birds have the best swing wings of all. A peregrine falcon holds its wings out to hover over its prey, then tucks them back to dive down for the kill. It can reach 200 miles an hour (300 km/h) in its dive.

● Harrier fighter planes have been nicknamed jump jets because they can take off straight up into the air.

Do airships run on air?

Modern airships should really be called gas ships, because they use a gas called helium to help them to fly. Helium helps airships to float because it is lighter than air.

The bag of an airship is called an envelope.

● Fairground balloons are usually filled with helium gas. To see which is lighter, helium or air, try holding a fairground balloon at the same time as a party balloon filled with air.

● The first air letter was carried by a balloon.

Burner

The first-ever balloon passengers were a rooster, a duck, and a sheep! Their 8-minute flight took place over Paris in 1783, more than 200 years ago.

Why do hot-air balloons float?

Balloons float because hot air rises, and hot air rises because it is lighter than cold air. The air inside a hot-air balloon is heated by a burner, which works rather like a camping gas stove.

Why do cars have wheels?

Cars and most other land machines have wheels because wheels make it easier to move. Things slow down when they rub against the ground. Wheels help because they turn easily, and only a small part of them touches the ground.

● Imagine how difficult it would be to move a car if all of it was touching the ground, instead of just its wheels!

● The world's longest car has 26 wheels. It even has room for a tiny swimming pool on board!

● Snow and ice are much more slippery than soil and rock. That's why skis and ice-skates don't need wheels.

Which are the biggest tires?

The world's biggest tires are made for huge dumper trucks, to cushion their heavy loads of rock and earth. The tires are nearly 12 feet (3.6m) high — that's about three times as tall as you are!

● The wheelbarrow was invented in China more than 1,800 years ago. It made it easier to carry heavy loads.

Which ships have wheels?

River boats called paddle-steamers are driven along by wheels. The wheels have wide boards called paddles. As the wheels turn, the paddles push against the water, moving the boat along.

Why do cars need gasoline?

A car needs gasoline for the same reason that you need food — to give it energy to move. It's hard to tell by looking at it, but gasoline has lots of energy locked up inside it. This energy is set free inside a car engine, so it can be used to turn road wheels.

● Many toy cars use electrical energy, stored in batteries. There are a few ordinary cars that run on batteries, too.

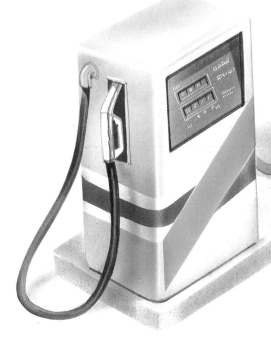

● Gasoline is made from oil, and it has energy because it comes from things that were once living! Oil formed millions of years ago, from the bodies of tiny plants and animals.

Exhaust pipe

Gasoline tank

● Gasoline is kept in a tank. It is pumped along a pipe to the engine.

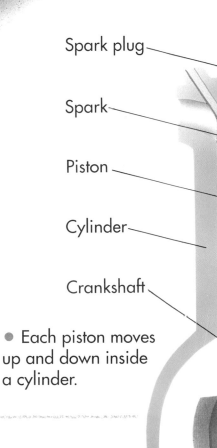

Pistons

● The world's biggest gas station is in Jeddah, Saudi Arabia. It has over 200 pumps!

What happens inside car engines?

Gasoline is mixed with air inside a car engine and then set on fire by an electric spark. This makes the air and gasoline explode with a bang. This explosion pushes engine parts called pistons up and down very quickly. The pistons make a rod called the crankshaft spin around. The crankshaft makes other rods spin, and they turn the road wheels.

Spark plug

Spark

Piston

Cylinder

Crankshaft

● Each piston moves up and down inside a cylinder.

17

Who cycled over the sea?

In June 1979, American Bryan Allen pedaled a special plane called the *Gossamer Albatross* across the Channel, from England to France, in just under 2 hours and 50 minutes.

Nine years later, Kanellos Kanellopoulos of Greece pedaled his *Daedalus 88* over the sea between the islands of Crete and Santorini.

Can bikes climb mountains?

Machines called mountain bikes are specially designed for rough stony ground. Their frames are extra-strong so they can stand up to rattling over bumps, while their knobbly tires grip well even in slippery sand or mud.

● It's not easy to balance on a unicycle — it only has one wheel!

How many people can ride on one bike?

● When the first bicycles were invented, about 200 years ago, they didn't have any pedals! People rolled them along by pushing against the ground with their feet.

Although most bikes are designed for one rider, special bikes are sometimes built to take more. The world's longest bike was built in Belgium. It had seats and pedals for 35 people, but it was very difficult for them all to balance and cycle at once!

How many people can ride on a motorcycle?

For more than two people to ride one motorcycle is difficult and dangerous, but there are stunt riders who do it for special shows. The members of an Australian motorcycling club put on an amazing display in 1987, for example. Forty-six of them managed to balance and ride on one machine!

● The first motorcycle with a gasoline engine was built in 1885. Much of the machine was carved from wood! It was destroyed by fire in 1903.

Which motorcycles have three wheels?

ATVs are special cross-country motorcycles, with three chunky wheels to grip and balance on rough ground.

- Some motorcycles are called choppers, because they have had bits "chopped off" and moved around to make them look unusual.

- ATV is short for All Terrain Vehicle. "Terrain" means land or ground.

Can motorcycles ever fly?

Motorcycles can't really fly because they don't have wings, but stunt riders still do amazing things on them. By speeding up a ramp and taking off from the high end, riders can make their machines leap huge distances through the air.

Why don't ships sink?

When things are put into water they make room for themselves by pushing the water aside. Although ships are heavy, they are hollow with high sides. This means they can settle quite low in the water, pushing a lot of it aside. In fact, a ship won't sink unless it is overloaded and becomes heavier than the water it pushes aside.

● You push water aside when you get into a bath. That's why you have to be careful not to overfill it!

How do submarines sink?

Submarines sink by making themselves too heavy to float. Water is let into special tanks to add weight. When it's time for a submarine to resurface, the water is pumped out.

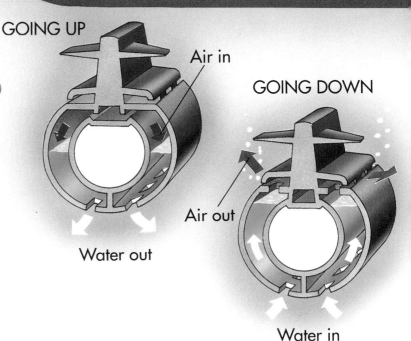

GOING UP

Air in

Water out

GOING DOWN

Air out

Water in

Which ships fly?

Although hovercraft travel across water, they don't float in it like ships. Instead, they hover just above the waves, held up by a cushion of air.

● Hovercraft can travel over land as well as water.

● This strange-looking diving suit was invented over 200 years ago. The tubes carried air to and from the surface.

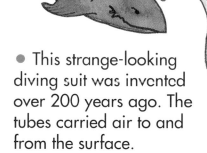

● One of the earliest submarines was built by Dutchman Cornelius van Drebbel and tested in the 1620s. Twelve oarsmen rowed a wooden boat below the surface of the Thames River, in England.

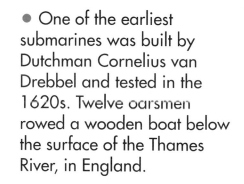

Which are the biggest ships?

The biggest ships in the world are oil supertankers. They can be over a third of a mile long and weigh more than 1,000 jumbo jets. Giant tankers can take 20 minutes to stop!

● Life jackets are only 200 years old. A French priest invented them when he lined a waistcoat with a floaty material called cork.

● Some tankers are so long that crews cycle around them!

What were longships?

We call Viking ships longships, although they weren't very big — less than 100 feet (30m) long. The Vikings lived in Scandinavia about 1,000 years ago. They built sturdy wooden ships and were skillful sailors.

● Viking ships could be rowed or sailed. They had a single square sail.

Which is the smallest boat?

Coracles are wicker-framed boats used in the British Isles. They usually have room for only one person.

- Warships once had small castles front and back.

Sterncastle

Forecastle

- Ships' hammocks were first used 500 years ago. European sailors copied them from hanging beds they saw in the West Indies.

Why don't trains fall off the rails?

Trains have metal wheels and run on narrow metal rails. Metal can be very slippery, so train wheels are specially shaped to stop them falling off. The inside of each wheel has a lip called a flange, which holds it on the rail.

Flange

Rail — Wheel

● The wagons rolled along at 1 to 2 miles per hour (1.5 to 3 km/h).

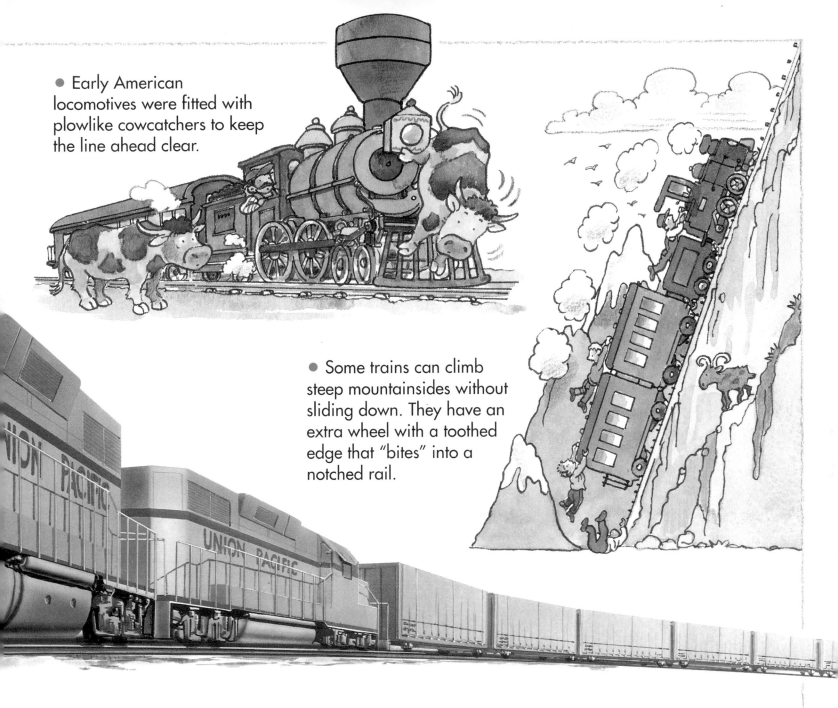

● Early American locomotives were fitted with plowlike cowcatchers to keep the line ahead clear.

● Some trains can climb steep mountainsides without sliding down. They have an extra wheel with a toothed edge that "bites" into a notched rail.

What were wagon trains?

In the 1800s, when settlers spread westward across North America, they took all their belongings with them in huge wagons drawn by oxen or mules. Families traveled in groups, their wagons following each other in a long line called a wagon train.

Do road trains run on rails?

No, road trains run on roads. They are called trains because they are made up of trucks pulling lots of trailers, in the same way that locomotives haul cars.

● Not all trains need drivers. Some city trains are controlled by computers.

● Australian trucks and cars often have strong metal bull-bars fitted in front to cut down damage if they hit large animals such as kangaroos or cattle on outback roads. Another name for them is roo bars ("roo" is short for kangaroo).

● Streetcars are buses with metal wheels that run on rails. They use electricity to move, taking it from cables stretched high above the road.

Bull-bars

● Road trains are often used in areas where there are no railroad lines — in parts of the Australian Outback, for example.

Can trains fly?

Maglevs are a kind of passenger train which float just above a special track. They are lifted and driven by the power of magnets, and they can travel very fast — at over 250 miles an hour (400 km/h)!

Which plane flies piggyback?

It's not every day that you see a plane riding piggyback, but it does happen. The Shuttle orbiter carries people into space and back again. When it returns to Earth from space it sometimes lands in California, thousands of miles from its takeoff base in Florida. To get back home again, it rides piggyback on a jumbo jet.

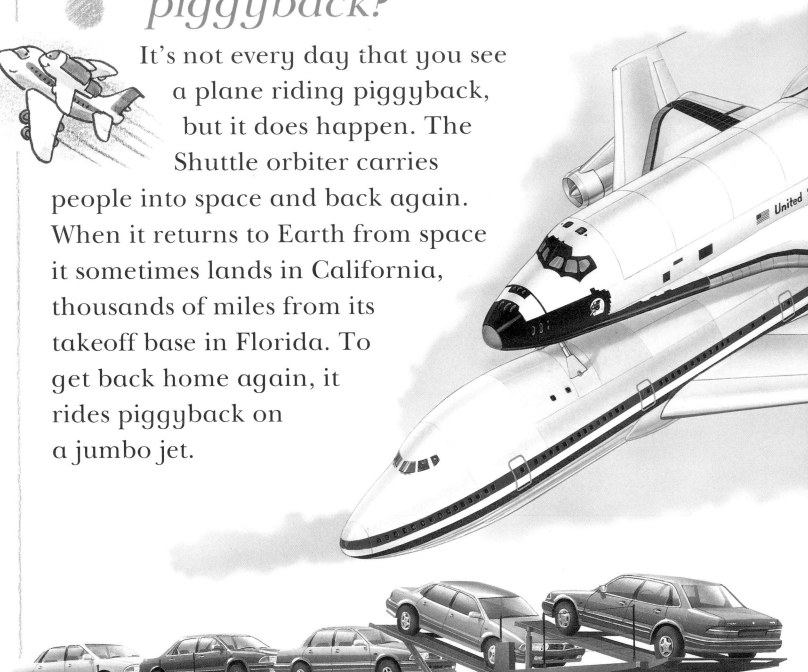

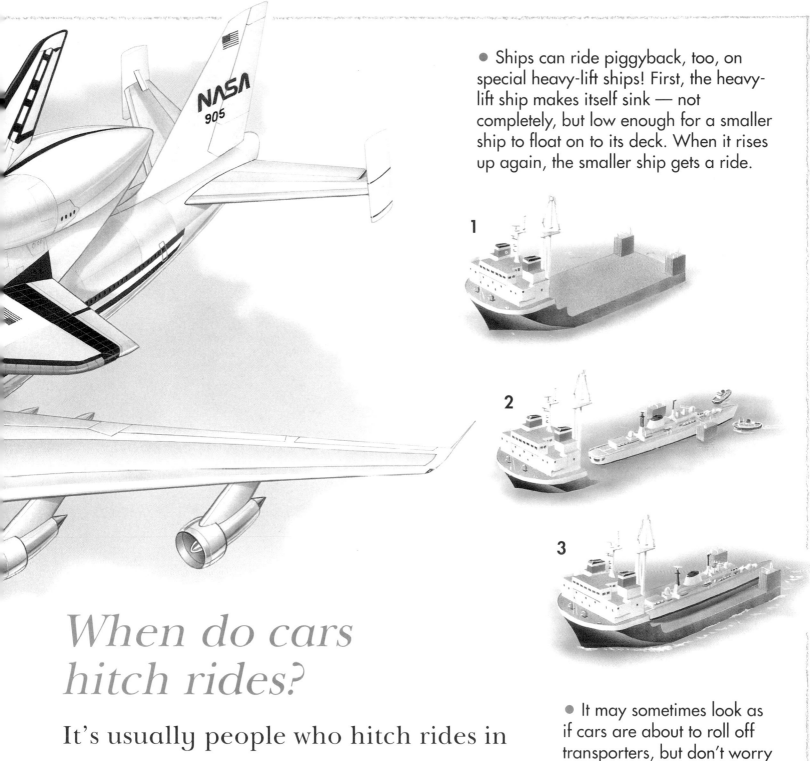

● Ships can ride piggyback, too, on special heavy-lift ships! First, the heavy-lift ship makes itself sink — not completely, but low enough for a smaller ship to float on to its deck. When it rises up again, the smaller ship gets a ride.

1

2

3

When do cars hitch rides?

It's usually people who hitch rides in cars, but sometimes cars themselves get taken for a ride. It happens when new cars are carried on trucks or trains from the factories where they are made, to showrooms where they are sold.

● It may sometimes look as if cars are about to roll off transporters, but don't worry — they're tied firmly in place.

Index

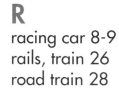

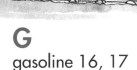

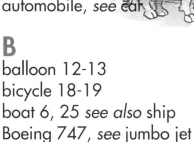

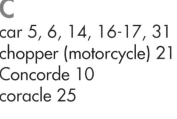